The
Lighter Side of
Technology
in Education

The
Lighter Side of
Technology
in Education

Aaron Bacall

CORWIN PRESS, INC.
A Sage Publications Company
Thousand Oaks, California

For information:

Corwin Press, Inc.
A Sage Publications Company
2455 Teller Road
Thousand Oaks, California 91320
www.corwinpress.com

Sage Publications Ltd.
6 Bonhill Street
London EC2A 4PU
United Kingdom

Sage Publications India Pvt. Ltd.
B-42 Panchsheel Enclave
New Delhi 110 017 India

Printed in the United States of America

Library of Congress Cataloging-in-Publication Data

Bacall, Aaron.
The lighter side of technology in education / Aaron Bacall.
    p. cm.
ISBN 0-7619-3802-8 (c. : alk. paper) — ISBN 0-7619-3803-6 (p. : alk. paper)
    1. American wit and humor, Pictorial. 2. Technology—Caricatures and cartoons.
3. Education—Caricatures and cartoons. I. Title.
NC1429.B127A4 2003a
741.5′973—dc21   2003040970

This book is printed on acid-free paper.

03   04   05   06   10   9   8   7   6   5   4   3   2   1

Acquisitions Editor:	Robert D. Clouse
Associate Editor:	Kristen L. Gibson
Editorial Assistant:	Erin Clow
Production Editor:	Diane S. Foster
Typesetter:	C&M Digitals (P) Ltd.
Cover Designer:	Michael Dubowe

Introduction

It all started somewhere between 1000 B.C. and 500 B.C. when the abacus was invented. Some 200 years later the zero was invented along with negative numbers. Mankind was off and running!

The summer before I entered college, I worked for a company that had a separate air-conditioned room that housed an immense Remington Rand UNIVAC computer. It's 5400 vacuum tubes took up 350 square feet—the size of some New York City rental apartments. That was my first look at a real computer, an outgrowth of the much slower and much larger ENIAC computer. That was my first introduction to the computer mantra, i.e., smaller and more powerful.

I purchased my first hand-held calculator for thirty-five dollars (my weekly salary) back in 1971 when the first microprocessor, the 4004 was produced. I was already behind the leading edge of technology.

It was all a blur after that. In 1973, Xerox introduced the Alto computer and the next year the 8080 microprocessor was produced. In 1975, Bill Gates and Paul Allen, two unknown computer enthusiasts, started a little company called Microsoft. Things moved fast after that. The next year the Apple was being sold and a year later the ubiquitous Commodore PET was introduced. All the while I was using my slide rule to solve complex problems in calculus, thermodynamics, and differential equations in college. That simple slide rule worked well for scientists and engineers for many years. The secret was to let your brain use it as a tool. That's the point. Although computers are ubiquitous, we have to remember that progress was made before computers by using the best computer in the world— the brain. Computers are only tools, although sometimes with a mind of their own.

Computer education in the classroom is important if we want to prepare students to be competitive in the world but we must remember that computers are tools to be used by educated individuals. There is no evidence that computers have increased academic achievement. The latter occurs through the hard work of dedicated, knowledgeable, and creative teachers who can fire up the imagination of youngsters.

Computers have profoundly affected all of our lives in countless ways, not the least of which is to sometimes frustrate and bewilder us. Read through this collection of cartoons and spot those familiar scenarios. We're all in this together. Have a chuckle.

—Aaron Bacall

About the Author

Aaron Bacall approached cartooning cautiously, stopping at college to pick up a degree in chemistry while drawing cartoons for the college humor magazine, then attending graduate school to pick up degrees in organic chemistry while drawing cartoons as he synthesized glutamate from histidine. All the while he looked for the quirky aspects in all he surveyed. He worked as an antibiotic research chemist and later as a teacher and principal curriculum writer for the New York City Board of Education. He has taught on the high school and college level. He is now a full-time cartoonist and humorous illustrator and is a member of the National Cartoonists Society and is on the Board of Governors of the Cartoonists Association.

His work has appeared in many publications, including *The New Yorker, The Wall Street Journal, Barron's, Saturday Evening Post,* and *Reader's Digest.*

His business cartoons have been displayed at the World Financial Center in New York City, and in 1977 he was awarded first place for the "Best Editorial Cartoon" by United Auto Workers.

To My Mother - Who didn't know what a computer was. She asked me if it could do nails and cut hair.

(Bill Gates, there's your next research project!).

To My Father - Who thought a computer was an expensive typewriter.

(For many computer owners, that's not far from the truth).

To My Wife, Linda - Who teaches computer courses in college.

(My computer password is ILOVEYOU)

To Darron - Who started with a 32Kb Atari computer

(And promptly learned how to use it and then devised some mathematical manipulations that he described in a paper that Atari published. Even then!)

To Barbara - Who sends me the cutest pictures of the cutest kids.

(I'll admit it, I'm biased!)

To Benjamin - A child of the Information Age.

(How did you work that mouse so well at age two?)

To Emily - A child of the Information Age

(A computer can do many things, but can it sing "Over The Rainbow" with style?)

COMPUTER DATING:
THE EARLY YEARS

"May I carry your disks to school?"

"Instead of observing your teaching, I'm going to install a Web cam in your classroom."

"I have a satellite link to the Naval Observatory. I receive a signal when the time is exactly 3:00 p.m. Then I'm out of here."

"The principal is keeping my teacher after school. She kicked the computer."

**"Although my hands *do* get dried out, a chalk
holder is not for me. I have technophobia."**

"We use these computers to gather and organize data for our school district and, on a slow day, to play solitaire."

**"Our computer teacher must be real old.
She remembers using Windows 3.1."**

"My class is so large and my seat
is so far back, I feel like I'm taking a
distance-learning course."

"There's no delete key. You have to use the board eraser."

**"Imagine if it were only this simple to upgrade
our staff."**

"It's an optical illusion. From the front of the room, they're all busy students working on computer projects. From here though, they're all busy playing Internet games."

"According to Einstein's theory, if we move the computer real fast, we can go back in time and recover the files you accidentally deleted."

"Sorry I'm late. I had to help the principal access her appointment schedule from her PDA."

"My teacher said my penmanship has really improved since I started doing my homework on an inkjet printer."

"Before I take my class on a field trip, I run through all the moves using virtual reality."

TEACHER, WHO CLAIMS TO BE KNOWLEDGEABLE ABOUT COMPUTERS, BLOWS HER COVER.

"You'll have to change your password. I was looking over your shoulder and I saw that you entered ******."

**"Timmy sent me e-mail from his hand-held
computer. He's locked in the boys' bathroom
and can't get out."**

"Here's your problem. You're using third-generation software but you're a first-generation computer user."

"The new teacher in *our* school is single and cute but he has commitment issues. He's changed his Internet service provider six times."

"I think I use the Internet too much. I find myself writing 'com' after each period."

"Due to recent technological advances, everything I taught you about computers is no longer valid."

"Rather than learning how to solve that, shouldn't I be learning how to operate software that can solve that?"

"Our school computers are one year old. How can they expect us to be competitive in the job market if we're being trained on obsolete equipment?"

"This book report is poorly written. Add some color and clip art, then resubmit it."

"Maybe you should replace the super platinum-iridium-cadmium batteries in your laser pointer with ordinary alkaline batteries."

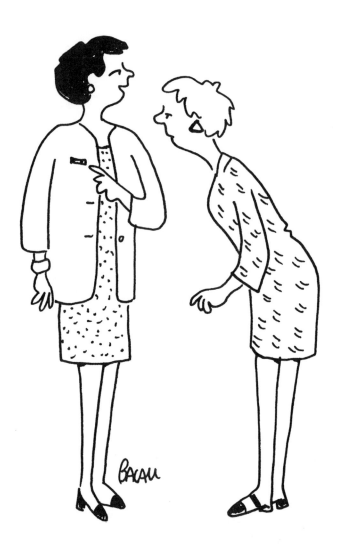

"It's not a designer pin. It's actually a medal the Principal gave me, for backing up my hard drive."

"If all the classes use computers, why am I still the eraser cleaning monitor?"

"Can I have the pass? I need to access the boys' bathroom."

"The software was free but the manual, the shipping, and the handling was two hundred dollars."

**"My computer froze. I wish my mom was here.
She carries antifreeze in the trunk of her car."**

"I'm sorry Benjamin, but the school is not prepared to exchange the take-home notebook computer we gave you for an electronic gaming system."

"My teacher said that if I disrupt the class one more time, she's putting your work number on speed dial."

"I started reading an online novel last night. It was so interesting, I just couldn't terminate the download."

"May I be excused? I just checked my college investment portfolio online, and I feel sick."

"I keep failing my spelling tests. I think my brain needs more RAM."

"Whoever is making the white noise, please stop."

"This spreadsheet program has really been enhanced since I installed the Ouija board."

"I don't have my homework because my dial-up modem couldn't connect with my on-line homework helper."

"Now it works fine. The computer must have had a twenty-four-hour virus."

"This must be your lucky day. You
have spam e-mail _and_ spam fax."

"This word processing program is *very* user friendly. All the O's contain a happy face."

"We ran into a glitch developing this new student data transfer program. It works well but we can't agree on a suitable acronym."

"This PowerPoint slide has a dynamic layout comparing reading scores throughout the district, which you would have seen if I remembered to bring a spare projection bulb."

**"Those are interesting questions Timmy.
I suggest you ask your search engine."**

"You have been cutting classes all term. I'm going to issue a computer tracking number to you, so I can know your location."

"Try rebooting."

"Yes, I downloaded my book report from the Internet, but I collated and stapled the pages all by myself."

"Can I talk to you offline?"

"Close the chat room and start your homework or I'll pull the plug and switch you to America Off-line."

"I switched from yoga to visualization, for relaxation. I picture a world in which all students with discipline problems attend my class online, from their homes."

"When I was a student, wireless data transmission meant passing notes in class."

"If you consider the time spent with tech support, our school's high-speed Internet access isn't that much faster than dial-up."

"I'm also in education. I issue bathroom passes for distance-learning students."

"I know my memos are looking a bit dated. I have to send for an updated version of the educational buzzword generator software."

"I downloaded music from a radio station in South Korea, and I got Seoul music."

**"It was easier when you went to school, Dad.
That was before the information age."**

"My son is away at college majoring in communication. When he sends me an e-mail message, I have to run it through the spell checker before it makes sense to me."

**"I can't keep up with technology. Just when I
finally learned how to use the fax machine
they come out with Internet faxing!"**

"Here's your problem. The software was manufactured in November and your computer was manufactured in February. Sagittarius is incompatible with Aquarius."

"I lifted the user's manual for this software with one hand and...."

"This biometric ID badge is part of the school's new security system. The badge contains my encoded retinal scan, fingerprints, and level of job enthusiasm."

"I called the 24-hour Teacher Tech Support Helpline but they were closed. Apparently they're open 24 hours, but not in a row."

"I didn't have time to download my report and print it out. It's already paid for, so *you* can download it directly from Book Reports-R-Us."

"This handheld computer is very useful for teaching. It displays my lesson plan, calendar, key files, and an extensive menu of put-downs for hecklers and classroom clowns."

**"If I need emergency assistance
with this program, do I type 911?"**

"When the school upgraded its operating system, for the third time, I upgraded my headache medication from over-the-counter to prescription strength."

"I'm Jeremy's father. I'm a computer consultant and I'm unemployed."

"He's a wizard. He came with the software."

"I warned you not to open that e-mail attachment. Three problem students were just transferred to your class."

"I stored all of my lesson plans in my notebook computer then backed them up by writing them in this composition notebook."

**"Emily, have you been shopping
online during class?"**

**"You've got 'parents questioning
a grade' mail."**

"I think Benjamin likes me. He linked my homepage to his homepage."

"I wrote a software program and sold it for two million dollars."

"Congratulations! This year we're saving money by letting all our graduates download their diplomas from our website."

**"We don't use screensavers in this class.
They use up too much memory. Try the
monitor's off button."**

"With a click of a key I can add objectives and a medial summary to each lesson plan. I wish it was that easy to add respect for teachers to each student."

"Giving each teacher a computer was a good idea, but why does the screensaver have to be a picture of the Principal staring at us?"

"This is our real-time chat room."

**CORWIN
PRESS**

The Corwin Press logo—a raven striding across an open book—represents the happy union of courage and learning. We are a professional-level publisher of books and journals for K-12 educators, and we are committed to creating and providing resources that embody these qualities. Corwin's motto is "Success for All Learners."